The love I met on the trail

샘문 시선 **1054**

Lee Jung Rok's collection Lee of poems

K-poetry

Bukcheong water seller's water backpack blows
through the dawn breeze
Which alley in Bukchang-dong?
An alley that sells cold noodles an ddumpilngs
Among the angle rafler in the old house covered
in grime, full moon rises round, round, round.
Before she knew it, her man was also on her chest

〈Gopdani, quoting part of the text〉

It's a place to dream
As I climb the bamboo forest path it is full of moonlight
Heard in the bamboo field

The pond is a place filled with moonlight
Golden moon water falls on lotus leaves with dew
The starlight joins in the dew
scatter the galaxy

〈 Bongchang , quoting part of text〉

The rumors they are talking about are
Who will record it?
Whether it's a tale or a legend,
that 2,000 - year - old guy, when crossing firing line
The guys next to him couldn't have even dreamed of it.
On the forbidden wall of the material world,
that guy draw strokes and dots to confine his life.
Passing over to the absolute world
It was a gamble and it would have been a companion

〈The reason yew trees have survived for 2000 years
, quoting part of text〉

Book publication **SAEMMOON**

*The love I met
on the trail*

The breathing sound of birth pangs

The feeling of republishing my first poetry collection, "Love I met on the trail," published around January 1993 after 30 years, is not only strange, but even magical.
The phoenix, the protagonist of the tragic story of Broken Wings, has grown wings little by little over the past 30 years, and is now shaking them off to ascend to space Grind the fine hair.
After rescuing clear and beautiful lyricism and beautifully sad love stories from the diagonal forbidden wall, he fills his stomach with bamboo shoots in the bamboo forest and sits on the vanish tree waiting for the red dawn.
The identity of the secluded being, the trace of life that were confined by drawing strokes and dots. Traversed this world, stayed in the diagonal line and then soared in reverse, climbing up to the top of the phenomenal world opening the door of perception from behind, returning to the naterial world and basking in a brilliant companion across the ray of dawn.
I tell the world that I hope that the eerie look in my eyes as I return home to the constellation of heaven, carrying my fleeting desires on my noble wings will be a sacred provocation.

Well then we are reborn, let's do some cuddles.
'What is poetry?' I asked this question 30 years ago too.
Like finding an answer to a question that everyone ecan ask but no one can Still on the line of verbal barbarism, as

Writer's Note

much as the star in the night sky scattered. I ask poetry again. There are about 15,000 poems, sijo, essays, columns and novels that I have Written in my spare time. In the mean time, I also made literary debuts in poetry, essay,
nobel, sijo and criticism. I received guidance from the late Midang Seo Jeong-ju at Bongsansanbang from around 1995 until his death and I also received guidance from Professor Lee Geun-bae, the current president of the National Academy of art of Korea, I also won numerous literary awards including the Korea Literature Award.

The Samteo Literary Award was established to award the main prize and the New Writers, awarding cash prizes, certificates, and plaques, providing stage performances and establishing two lifelong education centers to open the Department of Poetry Creation.
Department of Poetry Recitation, Department of Sijo Creation, Deppartment of Song and Department of Multi-Speech.
By receiving approval from government agencies to register private certification, we are discovering many future talent and train younger students.

This time I had the honor of being appointed as a head professor at Daelim University In themetropolitan area. They say becoming a university professor is picking star in the sky but I was appointed as a head professor in the Department of Leisure, Culture and Sports.
When it was announced that a poetry writing Department & a poetry recitation Department Will be established next year and that I will be appointed as dean, all of a sudden I had great happiness all at once.

Two years ago, I had the honor of being listed in the cultural and artistic figure section of the National Awards and Awards Dictionary complied by the National Awards Complication Committee.

I ranked 30th with legendary teachers Kim Dong- riand Park Mok-wol. I picked up my brush for the first time in 40 years and received special and honorable mentions in the Korean ink painting category at the international ZEN Exhibition (International Oriental Painting Competition) held at Tokyo Museum of Art in Japan(2017~2018).

I also applied the Korea Welfare Foundation and the Korea Creative Content Agency and was selected, so I received a lot of money and apublishing fee to publish a poetry collection.

But it still feels empty. Desire seems endless. I resolve, realize, and reflect everyday that I need to be more humble, humble myself, become less greedy, and be clean.

I hope and strive to become someone who respects and trusts myself by cleaning my mind through the poetry I have written from time to time and further refining the hardships and agony that must transcend and space along with the poetry that become a part of my life.

I pledge to raise my imagery, philosophy, and ideas to the highest level through thorough management to avoid contradictions and contamination of my own principle that should be written with a clear soul. I am trying to break through and innovate beyond the existing paradigm and realize the sample dream of becoming a grain of what for the board of directors but I am still hungry and dreaming endlessly.

Writer's Note

This time, I want to gather courage and want to become a freind who improves the Tao together . In order to live as writer in the future, I will have to go through endless hardships, but I plan to do my best to walk the path as a writer.

Although I may not be a phoenix whose wings flutter across the light. I may not a phoenix who eats bamboo shoots and does not anything other than the precious paulownia tree but like a skylark singing in the spring, like a cicada enjoying the summer, like a wildflower blooming in abundance in the field in the fall, even if it's an old tree full of snowflakes in winter, it's good, so I hope to do my best to write healthy articles that comfort and support everyone and myself.

Korea literary figures executives and members of Samteo Literature who gave me the courage to publish a reissued poetry collection and became my companion in literary activities Chairman Lee Geun-bae of the National Academy of Arts of Korea, International PEN Korean Headquarters Chairman Son Hae-il and Lee Gwang-bok, President of the Korea Writers Association, Chair Professor Jin-ho Lee , Chair Professor So-yeop Kim, Dr. Eun-Kyung Ji, advisors and instructor at Samteo College of Arts and Cultue, my beloved family and friends, the editorial staff of Samteo Literature and all my acquaintances. I would like to thank my only son, Treasure island. I would also like to say that I love and respect Lee Hyun-seok and Bijou Thank you everyone.

July 25, 1993
Samteo Lee Jung Rok

SAEMMOON | 1054

The Love I met on the trail
Lee Jung Rok - 9th Poetry Collection

The breathing sound of birth pangs / 5

Part 1 Plum flower, a Thousand Year of Love

The Sea That Dissolves Love / 14
River of Youth(Ceongchungaram) / 15
Companion / 17
Plum Flower, a Thousand Year of Love / 18
Love Song of Shepherd's Purse / 19
Hepatica in Snow / 20
Clownwort Witch / 21
Dandelion Love / 22
Peony / 23
Lyricism of May / 24
A Chick Dream of Spring / 25
Sprout Inside Me / 26
Lagenaria / 27
When Spring Day Comes / 28
When Spring Flower Fade / 29
When Spring Rain Falls / 30
Is Fireworks Beautiful? / 31
Thorny Red Rose / 32

Part 2 The Sun's Mistress, Wolgye

Peach / 34
Song of May / 36
The Sun's Mistress, Wolgye / 37
Queen's Solitude / 38
Bud / 39
Hesitation / 40
Butterfly Glasses World / 41
Self-Pollinator / 42
Late Summer Mountain Village Scenery / 43

A day of willow branches sway / 44
Desire / 46
Winter Daphne / 47
My Love Myeongja / 48
I will love you forever / 49
The magic of red roses / 51
Blue Ume Beauty / 52
Eternal Love / 53
Gourd Flower / 54

Part 3. Ah! Late Autumn, a Flaming Sunset

Moon Star Collaboration Ensemble / 56
Love is / 57
I Need To Go On A Trip / 59
Autumn, In Her Name / 60
The Last Leaf / 61
Red Rose Love / 62
Where Is My Heart? / 63
Song of Rich Year / 65
Ah, Late Autumn, Flaming Sunset / 67
Autumnal Love / 69
Swan / 70
Girl's Autumn Walk / 71
Autumn Is Gone / 73
Falling Flower / 74
Reed Flower / 75
Fallen Leaves / 76
Confessions of December / 77
Love Falls Like Snow / 78
Dream of Blooming Again / 79
Inherent Nature of Love / 80

Part 4, My Love, Sunae,Bo(Pure Love, Story)

My Love, Pure Love Story(Soonae, Bo) / 82
Love / 83
Wait / 84
Love of The Soul / 85
I Miss You / 86
Why Do We Love? / 87
go out to row alone / 88
Restraint and Freedom / 89
Forgiveness / 90
Bongchang(Small Paper Window) / 91
One Dream / 93
Gobdani / 94
One Dream / 96
Unstoppable Love / 97
Primitive Love / 98
Moon Bruce / 99
Sad Love / 101
Waning Moon / 102
Waning Moon / 104
Creative Love / 106

Part 5. The Reason Yew Trees have survived for 2,000 Years

Baby / 108
Hometown / 109
It's a Thatched Nest / 110
The Sound of Bier / 111
Childhood Friend / 113
Mother Is Getting Married / 114
Oh My Heaven! / 116
Flower / 117
One Dream / 118
Solitude / 119
Fishmen's Hope / 120
Moonlight Serenade / 121
Coexistence / 122
Contradiction / 123
Coincidence point / 124
Language of tears / 125
Silent Life / 126
Hunger / 127
Nameless Dump Flower / 128
Dreamlike Love / 129
A Letter Written in Silence / 130
The Reason Yew Trees Have Survived for 2,000 Years / 131

Part 1.
Plum Flower,
a Thousand Years of Love

The Sea That Dissolves Love

Look at that bronze sea where the starlight scatters.
It is pouring down brilliantly, carrying
the blue dream of the beginning
It is a song of the passionate love of
dissolving stars under blue longing.

Look at the white bronze sea where the moonlight scatters
Carrying the silver dream of the beginning
and crumbling desperately
Singing the passionate love of the moon
That casts a white longing and dissolves

Silenced by the lullaby of the stars, occasionally
Broken by the sound of the whale's sleep talking
The beloved mother who give birth dreams sacred
dream that all things desire.

That sea, as profound as the womb of goddess
endlessly repeats sacred and sublime creation and extinction
and comes waving the flag of sorrowful love.

Ah ~ Love,
Your pitiful and arrogant passion
I want to embrace you with the tentacles of instinct.

River of Youth(Ceongchungaram)

The sun also half down and sometimes buries
the face of clouds to cool off the heat
The golden beetle's skillful, gentle breeze
cools off the scorching heat
At cicadas's youth river, rehearsals for plenty song
of wild grains are in full swing

Before you know it, the flog melon are picked by moonlight
Body dressed in gold courtship
to fill babies in their bellies

Tired mind and body, I run to the water, soak my feet
In the flower river and pick up a watermelon to beat
the heat, pick up one or two books of poetry to kill time
and head the thatched-roofed pavilion under moonlight

If I am talken time off from my business life, tropical night
will put me to sleep. To the sound of starlings singing
autumn
I'm picking up my saggy thought.

On a fragrant night with a bittersweet scent

I walk step by step, measuring the distance.

Balman Balman(Step by step)

Companion

When I was having a hard time
you became my pain
and when I was sad
you became my tears.

When I was crying in pain on a tattered road,
In a humid swamp, the person who
became my frail breath and love me.

As the traces of my breathing prove,
The remaining moments also show
that I want you more earnestly
and that I love you more desperately
That's all the rest of my life.

The times when we can survive the world
without any hesitation we are together
and when we fail, we can get up
because we are together.

One day you came like sunshine
to my heart that was so miserable
As I can live with you,
I am happy today too.

Plum Flower, a Thousand Year of Love

A Plum tree covered in layers to withstand the harsh cold,
take off its coat and throw it way
and watery energy flowing through the bark
Soft eggplant with swollen, tender flesh trimmed,
twist every single knot and dye it
trimming the space of flowers,

How long they wait?
How did they hang around?

Spring breeze, walking along the river of sorrow love
Melody that blows one string at a time on spring night,
stamens are fluttering
Starlight love that enchants the soul
Moonlight love that moistens dry heart
Come quickly love
My love
Our love that will last a thousand years
will not end

Love Song of Shepherd's Purse

Angel
Plowing through the slightly melted snow
Did you have a hard time finding spring light?
From droopy shoulders to pale wings,
It's spring!

The brow of hill in grassy side
with friend who stick their heads out, Hello Greeting
A few tears falling
Does any other traveler look at you?
Come to pick you up, will you coming?
You will follow the spring sunshine

Don't worry
With a green smile and a bitter scent,
are you going to greet it?
Angel!

Hepatica in Snow

The spring snow still remains and in spring wind,
the collar is adjusted and the sunlight can't open the
side door
A girl quietly pry open paper window crevice
and draw a handful of sunlight
Prick up your fluffy ears and push up the remaining
snow
Open the upright flower stalk
Unleash your true feeling modestly
Love tempts me who is clumsy at
A longing buried in snow flower sorrow
A spring light walks in wearing flower shoes
Into the soft milky scent
A girl who gently tempts
It's blooming with spring love.

Clownwort Witch

You know what
What is that? You know that thing
You are the embodiment of spring
A pink halo is clearly emitted
It's a crucible of excitement
It's a flowing stream of color
that makes all the living being excited and dance.
Its not an ordinary monster.

You know what
What is that? You know that thing
Are you saying it's cutting off a lifeline, or are you saying it's fatal?
Anyway, you are like that
You are a magician who works strange magic
You are a white fox that uses tiny pink magic tricks
The spring wind has flown and the spring gost have awakened
It's not ordinary magic.

You know what
What is that? You know that thing
Yeah, a very pretty new bride
I mean, what's that?
Of course, that's right, your fan!

Dandelion Love

Loneliness rooted between isolated stones.
Simplicity approaching with a bright smiles
Detachment clumsily embracing the dew
A white universe conceived with greasy tears
A single seed of colorless life!
You fly away on the breeze of the grass
Some where, in which field or on which road
A lonely new spring will bloom
and it will convey the longing that
wiil be remembered in the future

Like a desperately flowing river,
Our love was heartbreakingly sad
and like a baby's eyes, it was beautiful
and sublime ~

Peony

Our meeting is warm,
Like my heart, like your pure heart
A goddess who flutters like angel
A goddess with a white jade fragrance

Not ten or a hundred
It blooms as just one flower
On the trail filled with lover's scent
Flowers that light up the lamp

Lyricism of May

The bank in the heart of mountains are filled with green water
which is overflowing and brimming
mountains and valleys are dizzying heights and lows
stem of ordeal, leaving a temporal and spatial gap.

The peach blossom and apricot blossom on the ridge
are burning a thill of passion.
and the garden where spring has left
is colored with a fresh green scent.

The cicada in the cocoon is embroidering
preparing the flapping of wing
The hot sun of passion is polishing it's voice to sing
May is busy every day
The valley of the forest is always full of the scent of pine

As the moon rises and wind blows coldly
My empty heart is filled with longing
but pine needles fan the moonlight beautifully
and welcome the traveler.

A Chick Dream of Spring

Beyond the border of the winter stream,
The wind blowing from the thawing color of water
is quite chilly
In a languid spring day that covet it's shivering wounds,
fluff down between the two wings of it's mother's arms
is also warm.

The starlight that drives away the harsh energy
and shines in the darkness
pecking with its delicate beak, moon rises
clinging to the mother's beak, flapping its wings dangerously
standing at the starting line for the beginning of life.

A world where it dream after its mother
singing and dancing and talking a sip of the sky blue
A dream raised with eye looking at the sky
In the warm wings of spring inside it,
A sprout of hope sprouts

Sprout Inside Me

The wind blowing from the thawing color of water
is quite bitter.
On a languid spring day wrapped in bitter taste
The embrace of afaint dream is hazy

Driving away the harsh energy
a cluster of stars in the darkness
open my eyes as they peck with their beak
The element of life, a galaxy that scatters,
a light green being ovulates
The full moon warm up and pours out moon water.

In a world that dreams like a dream
Drinking the color of sky and using reed, yellow, blue paints
A being raised by drawing landscapes
Build a nest inside me.

Lagenaria

Tempting the spring sunlight
the flower stalk is in full bloom

Spread out your red heart
becoming the incarnation of woman

Bright red cheeks and lips
Light up like a red lamp.

When Spring Day Comes

If snow flower sheds tears in the spring breeze,
my lover will follow the spring breeze too

When the delicate flower buds stay in the eye of beautiful spring sunlight
my lover follows the spring sunshine too.

When the sadness in the flower buds matures into longing
my lover come follow longing too.

Even if the faint dream light is wind that disappears when waking up
My lover follows the spring road in dreams too.

When Spring Flower Fade

Was this waterway, lying down with kind eyes,
a river of sorrowful love that you and I had rowed
with our eyes?

Resenting moon for holding breath
Hang it bronze starlight heart,
Looking for traces of the weft of Nakhwa Rock,
A thousand miles path, compassion throws away
Flower skirts flutteringly. Hovering water light

Still the fateful road that must be walked
The flower petal boat that sadly separates last love.
Welcome my lover.
Floating along the water for a thousand miles, taking deep breath
Following the traces of my reverberations.

When Spring Rain Falls

Cold snow which had been shivering from the snowy wind all winter
is swept it's heart by the spring breeze and soon sheds tears
Are they spring snow's tears?

The spring rain sheds tears
moistens the empty branches of bare trees.
To burst flower buds for new shoot bloom
soak them with moisture.
Setting up light green eyes,
Blooming buds smile brightly
Spring rain of hope...

When thus rain stops,
the green buds will grow even more.
Every branch of bare trees
Will bloom flower buds
The spring breeze will make the skirt flutter,
will delivered the fragrant scent of spring to my lover!

Is Fireworks Beautiful?

Does life ultimately boil down
to love that perishes?
like a burning red sunset.

Does love burn and perish soul?
like the moonlight that burns white and fades

Life is a finite flame
and love is also a glimmer of flame
that blooms and falls within it

Thorny Red Rose

Will she become a sharp knfe and piece the heart?
Will she become a soft needle and embroider love?
She raise he rtentacles tightly

A powerful thrill
A trembling in my chest
a painful love that swallows you up with a neck
that bends as if you can barely breathe
A sunset tern blood red.

It's love
All of this will be love
The pain, joy, and longing she feels
all of this will be love.

Clever temptation
Seeing a burning hope
Even keen insight

Part 2
The Sun's Mistress, Wolgye

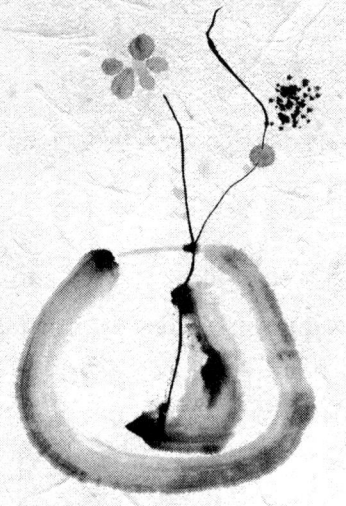

Peach

Sunlight between peach trees
in the waving hands of green leaves
crumbles small

During the peach blossom season, bee and butterfly are loud
The day when the strong flower wind blew
leaving knotted marks due to child birth
Peach blossoms with beautifully flower stems
swell their scarlet breast and
are busy preparing themselves for marriage
Vamp kept sexually excited sunlight in her mouth
A woman who captivates traveler's soul
The front is pretty
The back is pretty
until overflowing rain dew all night long
Is it that pretty?

Something that looked like a fairy's breasts
Something like the soft insides of a first love
In a neat and tidy ,pure love!

It giving all the love of a stork
It's nice to be immersed in the whispering
Such a heart-fluttering moment
Where else is it?

Into scarlet love
It is snugged into your white

Song of May

Longing is shaken to overflowing in abyss.
Thoughts are dizzy, high and low.
and is crying violently. It is May.

Peach blossoms and apricot blossoms are exquisitely beautiful
Lush green of greens that has passed the passion
Full of fresh green. It is May

Embroidering their wings in cocoon
and polishing their voices with burning passion,
Grass cicadas are busy everyday, It is May.

Acacia love is a hazy love
You intoxicated with the scent of pheromone
and fall into my arms
Full of blue dreams. It is May.

Gourd Flower Beauty

Between the thatch eaves of thatched fence,
A meiden lady wrapped in white cotton clothes
Look at the sunset and smiles shyly.
It is more simple and beautiful than
the peach blossoms rowing in a flock of the moon
Wild rose that hide tentacles at foot of the mountain and flutters
more simple and beautiful than Haeeohwa
that are loved by the king in the old royal palace.

The sound of loud laughter, sparkling in the rising moonlight .
Sunset hidden in the ridge of mean cottage
Chewing cranchily
Coming with a blue lantern on
Smile at stars.

* Wolgyeihwa : Wild rose
* Haeeohwa : A beautiful flower that understands human speech
* Nuok : A shabby but comfortable

The Sun's Mistress, Wolgye

Late summer skirt
The sky blue wild rose's fragrance
Is carried by the early autumn wind
and sweeps the tip of mt nose.

A woman who longed for the sun
and allowed herself her body
and stands alone at the corner of mountain foot
chasing the longed sunlight
resenting the clouds

A traveler who urge on his way
waiting for the autumn color
The red figure of the woman
Take hold of the steps.

Queen's Solitude

At the end of May
The greenery has already become lush.
It sems like early summer.

On a rainy day of growth and vitality
The red pity in my heart I s throbbing

One year, the bloody feast of rose vines
Unfold
The longing that departed in the spring rain
after the covenant ceremony

At this time as I wander around the edges of my mind
The pity that has subsided, palitate once again
The rhyme of waves flows down my spinal cord and
The hunger of deep abyss is gathering.

A time of remorse and lamentation
The lotus that was baked the swamp,
The swaying and embracing
spleen's faint groan is heartrending

Bud

Mountains and river crying in the cold wind,
memories of the past are scattered and swept by the empty wind.
the empty valley is filled with only empty winds.
In the fields where the spring rain has stopped,
a new wind blowing with the fresh scent of spring

You woke up in a flash
to the sound of a blue star sparking brightly
the delicate gestures of a butterfly quietly visiting,
your quivering eyes,
moist lips, a rich scent blooming

What now?
Spring has come, so like newly grown stem of green,
Will the bud of love in your heart bloom?
I'm looking forward it.

Hesitation

"The light pink skirt was blowing in the spring breeze"
A verse of a verse of a melodious song unintentionally
flows out of the poet's mouth.
Why?
Why suddenly?
Is spring coming in a corner of his heart?
Is it pity for a lost love?
Or is it affection for new love?
Spring, fluttering and falling
on the bridge of the nose
He quickly grabs a handful and squeezes it
The sound of light green new shoots
the trembling of the tender flower buds
awaken the poet's imagination as spring approaches

Butterfly Glasses World

From the bridge of my grandfather's nose
to the bridge of my father's nose,
sitting quietly and swaying

A curious butterfly flying quietly
suddenly gets on a roller coaster
and lands on the bridge of my nose.

The world is spinning round and round
sky is shaking and falling
and her drunken dance moves
The two world are spinning crazy.

Self-Pollinator

It's hot fever
The storm of passion is heading toward you
with a hot confession.
and long for you without hesitation.
A condensed heart vomit hot wet dream
It's an unstoppable love,
a violent wave.
Two souls unite.
With all their heart and souls
They love passionately

[Quotations by Samteo]

Flowers are also born in the world
Love and reproduce between opposite sexes

All things with a warm heart love someone between the sexes This is an expression of inherent instinct.

It is not an emotion that can be supperessed by suppressing it but a special blessing from God.

Late Summer Mountain Village Scenery

A mountain village getting wet
and catching its breath
A pair of cicadas that were whining wetly
and playing hot love games,
a flock of crows that were squealing loudly
are buried in the sound of the rain.

In the last warm sunlight
The melons that were roasting naked
are turned blue and scattered around in surprise.
Ants under a maple tree wander around the entire mountain
and hide in a hole in the ground at three or four drops of rain

Telling us to rest for the final fruition
Crossing the boundary of the cycle,
heavy rain of the last season
wetted the evening
and the mountain village soaked
was steeped in a cozy and sweet rest
into cot corn stalks.

Ugly You

A day of willow branches sway
Shall we hold hands with you, my ugly lover
and go on a flower outing to fields and mountains?
Shall we pick azaleas and play flower rice pancake?
Shall we have a daytime drink with ripe cherries

Here! I am here and I have drinking too!
Have a drink and you look lovely
Our spring outing is fun!

Desire

I want to give you spring in the palm of your hand,
So I made it with the sincerity I gathered from the fields.

This is a chest created by blowing hot breath
away from the strong wind.

I hope that a smile with a deep scent
in the flowing hot blood
will be conveyed to you.

It's spring
the day you've been waiting for so long...

Winter Daphne

The beginning of spring has passed, when jars break
and even though, Jack Forest angry,
winter daphne which burst out beautifully and indifferently

An elegant purple chima, a pure white Jeogori,
a gesture that the spring of hope is coming and
auspicious water scent announce it to a thousand mile
Like your confession, the love in dream awakens
and flaps wings span a thousand mile.

The miracle of love happens
The luck of love comes to me
The scent of love flies a thousand miles
And wake up my sleeping five senses
With a stimulating and intense body odor,
winter daphne who tempts me into my dreams.

Chima - Woman's Skirt of Korean clothing
Jeogori- Woman's Jacket of Korean clothing

My Love Myeongja

I am happy because of you
A woman who urges the red sunlight to crimson quickly
Myeobgja looks more mature than a poppy.
Riding on the fluttering spring breeze.
In every branch and every knot
bloomed a flower of passion.

My heart flutters at the sight of you.
A woman colors the moonlight aura in crimson.
Myeongja who looks humbler than a rugose rose.
My soul is broken,
buried in your eyes
I'm looking at you coldly.

I will love you forever

On this deepening autumn day
I feel you with my whole heart.
I embrace you full.
I smile with joy all the times at the clear sky.
Our kiss melt into
Sweet cotton candy.

Pretty memories to fill my swollen heart
You who only think of good memories.
You who have a dreamy smile and a tearful look over flowly
Following the excitement that catches your eyes
Following the longing that reaches out a warm hand.
At the sunset mountain lodge,
the autumn colors of the brown and scrimson colors
burn out, the sad love struggles

My song is a song of pure autumn
A song of blood sung by a thorn bird
I confess to you.
I love you.
I love you and I will love you again
I will love you forever.

[Samteo Quotations]

The sensuous love you feel
can not be achieved through an artificial
approach and is like fate that comes by
chance.

[Samteo Quotations]

Beautiful love is an unaffected, nature-
friendly love steeped in the emotions of
nature, purity and compiliance.

The magic of red roses

In a half-asleep, moonlit, doctrinaire night,
a passionate kiss,
crimson lips fumbling
I got caught in a tentacle.

My thoughts are intoxicated by her halo
and I fell into a fever.

Is it magic?
Are you a wizard who was possessed by magic
And trapped in a red skirt?

When I woke up from a dream, I was a dream again
and when I opened the trance, I was a trance again.
and the thing and self became one.
and it was a spring dream.

The butterfly in her dream bring her thrilling adoration
between heaven and hell
from her stem.

My self goes round and round endlessly
Looking for her scent in the maze.

Blue Ume Beauty

The scent of plum blossoms is just breathless joy.
The freshness of plums is your withered and emaciated soul.

Water mist rises and on a moist morning
Every branch of trees that has risen water
Your heart hangs jureongjureong(in clusters)
approaching as cheongmaegain(Blue Ume Beauty).

From well-rounded dew to the glimmer of sunset
It comes with a sour breath
Taenggeul, taenggeul
with blue-green love

> Cheongmae Gain : Blue Ume Beauty
> Jureongjureong : the appearance of many fruits hanging on the tree.
> Taenggeutanggeul : Fruit is plump and round in shape .

Eternal Love

There is no a dream garden anywhere in the world.
Let me decorate it
I will decorate it with your flower bed
And it will bloom all year round in the name of flowers.

I will become your poem, your song, and your star,
and on a mist moonlit night
I will pour down and sink into your heart.

I will plant my roots tightly in your heart
and grow you into a star flower that conforts
and cheer you on after suffering from love

I wiil touch your heart with obedient wordplay,
embrace the sky with passionate energy, give birth to clouds,
call for rain and make star flowers bloom.

I will soars high as a flower stem with a serving heart
and a falling flower like a meteor.
sit on your heart
and become a knot that testifies
to eternal love.

Gourd Flower

A woman who draws clear water in the early morning,
put fresh water on the stove,
kneels neatly
and prays with all her heart.

The pale white color
is a pure beauty that blooms in solitude,
a pitiful beauty that eerily attracts the heart,
a woman with tears of sorrow.

When everyone else is a sleep,
a sad mother-like woman who blooms at night.

Part 3
Oh Late autumn, Flaming sunset

Moon Star Collaboration Ensemble

After an all-day struggle, sunset which has survived
the day, puts down evening sub.
The moonlight greet them politely
and starlight, that followed unexpectedly
plays a soft opuscule to the tune of
collaborative eyes of the ensemble friends.

When the black space-time is emptied
and the silence implied by condensation is filled.
the serenade of scops owl beautiful and sad,
owl's blue eyes trims darkness and
illuminate the silence.

Bright supia moon gently pulled and soaked the moonlight
and thirsty heart suckles the nipples of
star flower.

Supia : Forest fairy

Love is

The slow misty rain
moistens the newly bloomed flowers,
but my love is very slow,
trapped in that roaring curtain
and doesn't know how to escape.

For example
when love comes,
it comes like the wind,
blooms hot like a flame ,
and soaks in moisture like misty rain.
When love goes,
It wets the collar like a rainstorm,
and is taken away like a ebb.
The flower stalk vomits blood and blooms
The stamen is very sad because of intense love
The flower-colored flower glands are blooming in abundance

A fearful yet exciting love that comes quietly
like the core of typhoon,
a desperate love that is trying to protect itself

from being extinguished.

Love is
Love is
protecting

Love is
like that

I Need To Go On A Trip

One day, in the autumn
I will go on a trip with you
and go wherever my feet take me.

On that day, it will be nice not to
have to carry the burden of having
to meet someone or do something

Sky and earth look different than usual,
and I want to meet our living love,
singing a song of hope with a heart
that feels like it's about to fly.

I have to leave.
I have to leave to see you.
I need to go on a trip this autumn.

Autumn, In Her Name

Is it the season to call a man?
A woman giving birth in rd of whole mountains
with swelling autumn color pure love ovulated.

Forest of ripping five-colored waves,
exhaling rough breath,
scattering the pain of withering

Her brilliance blends in with indigo color,
making her in to beautiful woman,
and the thrill of combined passion
pierces the clear sky and heaven's fragrance.

If you brush against it, it releases a scent,
If you touch it gently, it turns red,
and if you tap it, it blooms.

The season of ripe love
Calling the man,
her name is autumn

The Last Leaf

As it rains
a leaf dangling from a bare branch
is trembling.

Oxidizing tragic hero
weeps

A fate that it doesn't know when!

Whole soul's taillight, fading soul!
squeeze its rough chest and swallow its tears of blood

How will it survive this night?

That leaf
Heart aches...

Red Rose Love

She, who want to love, unfolds slightly
and is embraced with trembling gesture
with a red temptation
with a blood-red covenant

She had a deep tentacle to protect her purity
but her delicate breasts were covered in fresh blood
due to the passing May winds

In a moist moonlit night
she burst open her closed pistil
with the pain of passion that was like the spring sunlight.

She had a bright smile on her face all morning
and expressed her love
with a red love letter, right?
God of Flower!

Where Is My Heart?

Faced with white snow,
lighting up in ray of spring sun light,
I waited for newly grown stem.

Making eye contact with flowers
I found a blue-green green

The parched, breathless fresh green,
Its eyes are faltering
It was lost

Where will it go?
Where can it go to find it?
Where did it go?

Now let's go
Aja Aja!, let's go
To the place where autumn breeze dance
the lower night sky opens the stage in my arms,
wind and clouds whisper
The song of a moonlight melody...

Sonata of little stars
Serenade that colors the mountains and fields
is Garam there dancing
the sliver dance?

Aja Aja : A sound shouted by people in the same situation to encourage them to overcome each other or a sound made by an encouraging person shouting to the other person to overcome well.
Garam : Old word for river or lake

Song of Rich Year
− Wonang Sori (Sound of cow's neck bell)

The sound of farmer's Woi, Woi plowing
the paddly field is lovely
Sound of arrow cow's bell is like Yukjabaegi rhythm
The basket of snack on woman's head
Is dancing flutteringly

The clap back sound of cuckoo is drooping in west mountain.
and one Majigi next to the pit is plowing until sunset,
but arrowroot cow is foaming at the mouth and plow hard
and do something else. Farmer is getting into a stew and his mouth
smells. When west twilight is creeping up the bare mountain,
The spine of mournful farmer's wife get wet,
cotton jacket is damp.

Ehera Jihwhaja
If farmers sing rich year's song in autumn
Oxen, farmers! Eogiyeongcha be strong!
Woman's Farmer song were rich and cool

and dance to rhythm of basket
Autumn breeze cools down cotton jacket.

The arrow-root cow plowed completely
and its Wonang sound echoes through the field
Grains of five grains are hanging jureong jureong
and in the a golden field waiting for havest,
they sing the song of rich year.

Wonang : Neck bell of cow
Yukjabaegi L : Farmer's song when plowing
Majigi : Korean farmland traditional meadurement
(1 Majigi= 671.57 SQM)
Eherajiwhaja : A sound made to the tune of song or dance to arouse exicitement
Jureong jureng (Hanging in clusters) : The appearance of many fruits hanging

Ah, Late Autumn, Flaming Sunset

A breathtakingly beautiful sunset flows
as if you can reach it if you stretch out your hand
but stays for a while as if it's sad.

"Love and life must be as fierce as you are"

As autumn wind screamed in awe,
echo came back with sunset.
Into the red leaves of all mountains, where passion erupts
at the last moment, before I knew it, it had seeped
A yearning autumn
The pity I embrace until it's crushed
The red tears of confession
blooming with remembrance

The fading autumn sunset!,
swaying autumn wind,
burning red leaves
I'm so excited that tears are flowing
A frame buring in the heart of red-brown autumn color

live fiercely until it runs out of breath

Become a handful of ashes and be held
in the arms of your loved one
love until the end

[Samteo Quotations]

Life is ultimately a love that dies.
Like the red-burning sunset , love also
burn s the whole soul and dies Life is finite.
The love that blooms within it is also

Autumnal Love

Even if autumn breeze passes by gently
tears are flowing on the leaves
My longing love

My thin, trembling heart
Is embraced by the red sunset glow
My longing love

A heartbreaking confession of a stained heart
I will keep the words that I love you.
My longing love

Swan

Angel made from feathers of feathered clouds
You are a flower more beautiful than the white water lily,
the flower of flowers.

When you kick the water and fly
I envy the stylish, sensual gestures
that the swaying light colors.
and the lake is submerged in big eyes of white water lily.

A flower that blooms whiter than pure white snow.
and swims while embracing the purity of the waves
You are a pure white saint.

Be comforted by your gesture of love.
water lilies shimmering with whiter flowers
are the only longing you gave me.

Girl's Autumn Walk

A pretty girl walk along the forest path,
her pure innocence is moist and moist under autumn sunlight,
her breast adjusted pus of clothes, are shaking
flowers are fragrant and lovely

Autumn trees in five-colored jacket,
chattering river
dancing of burning red leaves
a pretty girl flashing a bright smile.

A girl lightly steps on the maple leaf, five-colored flower shoes,
and walk up pine tree path sapoonsapoon(with soft steps)
the chipping mountain birds
are holding leaves in their mouths like girl's red skirt.
and flapping their wings in blessing.

Five-colored leaves are flying
Spring water of puddle is gushing songsongsong
and flowing around the rocks
Acorns are rolling in droves(ddegulddegul) and acting

cute.
Baby squirrels are laughing delightly
and the plants are dorandoran happy

Autumn forest with brown jacket
It matches girl's beautiful figure
and paradise is spread out
floweriness, beauty, burning mountain ridge,
she climb into lover's arms.

> Sapoon sapoon : Waliking with steps so light that no sound is made
> Song song song : Shape of water rising
> Ddegul ddegul : Obeject keeping rolling
> Doran doran : Sound of speaking politely in a low voice

[Samteo Quotations]

The coexistence of nature and human
is a harmonious blessing
The love that blooms within it becomes
a beautiful and beautiful legendary flower.

Autumn Is Gone

Is the sunset sad,
the wind sad, or
the moonlight sad?

Does that water color, which oxidizes and rusts,
know sorrow?

Does that leaves, which wither and fall,
know sorrow?

Does your cool heart know sorrow that flows
from eyed look of falling autumn?

Falling Flower

The road you take is a flower road
and the stairs you climb are flower stairs.
Can it be beautiful with love?
The beautiful lights and scents
This road of five colors feels like
A wall blocked by the wind.
My heart aches. I am wandering
around unable to step on the sad flower path
as you are trampled upon
by my eyes

Reed Flower

Are only spring flowers
flowers?
Even the falling leaves of
a single leave was a time
when the red leaves of all
mountains were splendid.
The earnestness of thing
depend on the gaze of the beholder
and the heartbeat differently
In the poet's eyes,
even a single red leaf
appears to be a flower.
So it is worth seeing
It as a flower.

Fallen Leaves

A pomegranate-colored sunset is burning
and river breeze that boils with longing image
To soothe the sadness of separation,
a single-leafed boat was floated.

In the melody of water color scattered by the underwater
full moon, Maybe, lover's scent is carried
As the waves wave, as the wind blows
Sareureureu sareureureu
 It splits the river water

Sareureu, sareureu : Quite and smooth movement

Confessions of December
- God is Love

It's a beautiful companion
It's a happy December because I'm with you.
There's not much time left this year
I hope you will a successful end
with the joy of being with the person
you love, me.

Greeted with a warm heart,
coming new year,
let's hold each other in our arms for a hopeful new year,
you and I go back to the beginning,
growing old together and buried in the same grave,
I want this to be the first year of a long journey
It's my wish

I confess to you
I love you,
I love you as much as death.

Love Falls Like Snow

It's snowing
When the sky opens and snow falls.
The world is full of silver waves.

A pure white world where nothing has been removed,
A longing that is like white drawing paper that can not be drawn,
With a scribble of heart-pounding confession,
I am afraid I'll get wet with your thoughts.

I beg as much as the amount of large snow flakes
that has fallen and erased the boundaries of the sky

Just like the color of pure white snow,
as much as the color of the white pum blossoms
that bloomed with snow flower's tears,
I will love you.

On the slender shoulders, a wretched snow flower
is tembling with love and longing

Dream of Blooming Again

You, who want to give everything,
are less heart broken because you are holding the light of
profound dream, Even though you have a hard time
with trials and discouragement now,
you will rise up and move forward with strength.

I am not worried about you who are full of hope.
Even if you are suffering now, you who wriggle with
upright faith, will soon be loved by many being.

You always have a clear face and full of smile
Don't worry
You look pitiful now and your upright nature
will bring joy to the ego that has lost It's dreams
and become the center of a happy world.

You know how to be satisfied with small things.
Don't worry
Although it may seen foolish now,
the plant in your deep forest
will bloom flowers called success.

Inherent Nature of Love

That
is a primordial scared sanchtuary
that can not be violated by any
rules, laws, procedures or formalities.

That
has a mysterious power
that can eliminates any difficulties and dangers
and an absolute magical power
that defies gravity

That
is a source of life flows endlessly
from the spring of the beginning,
no matter how much you consume.

That
conceives and dissolves the universe,
grows and blooms.

That
is why it's so great.

Part 4
My love,
Pure Love Story(Sunae Bo)

My Love, Pure Love Story(Soonae, Bo)

Waiting for the rising moon
I dozed off and wandered in my dreams

While making the moon,
At the sound of little cuckoo's breath cry,
I swept my heart way.

I picked a star to give you
and lost my mind in your backside
taking a bath in the Milky Way River far way

Love
Soonae, Bo for you, I went for a short walk
Don't be disappointed and welcome
My eternal flower star

Love

Love is a wizard with supernatural powers.
Love is an alchemist with taoist magic and
a supernatural that can transcend
the limit point, the critical point.

Love, sometime,
falls in front of your eyes
with enchanting, streamlined sensuality
with a splendid appearance on white horse.

Love, sometimes,
a magician that lifts the weary body and mind
to the realm of virtue on high level
and manifests, realizes anything
with a miraculous inner strength.

Love is ever-changing, and
more beautiful than flower, more frangrant than flower,
and is a perfumer who always mixes
and scatters.

Wait

Autumn wind blows in a lonely houses in the lake.
and autumn leaves turn red.

My heart is also turned red
at the thought of lover

Mt earnest love is
still not coming now
but are you coming in a dream?

Love of The Soul

Sublimated love is infinite

It flows endlessly, going back and forth
between the time and space of life and death.

It oxidizes into a single point of light
and is pierced into the heart.

Blooming as
a heart-fluttering flower.

I Miss You

I miss you
and the day is coming to an end
On days when the day feels long
it's a day when I miss you so much
When people meet and become close
longing rather than love
comes to mind first.
I miss you
not because you are far away
but because I can't see you when I want to see you
I miss you again today
and the day is coming to an end
I am hungry
because I miss you
My eyes hurt
because I miss you.

Why Do We Love?

People know that if they break up after loving,
they will be deeply hurt,
but why do they love?

Isn't it because they want to make sure
that they are not alone?

go out to row alone

Love is
hanging a lantern on a flower stalk,
filled with the covenant of dream light.
You and I singing
going to meet the moon.

Love is
listing to a song of sorrow for the moon
in the melody of the water orchestra.
You and I becoming one
confessing while looking at the stars

Restraint and Freedom

Love is
not restraint
but rather a liberation from
loneliness, solitude, and self-righteousness.
flying toward home
empty and consume
shake off your hands,
returning home to my fixed star

Forgiveness

I need to let go of the wound
before the knots grow
before the roots take root

I shouldn't hold on any longer
How can I let go?
Hate but comfort,
Is that the best way to let go?

I have to let you go with tears of compassion
Hurt and grace are incompatible
So I have to shake off all the love and hate.

I shouldn't wait until I atone.
Forgiving and comforting the hurt
Is pardoning for the sake of love,
I should live selfishly

Bongchang(Small Paper Window)

It's a beautiful place.
It's a place where the light changes like magic.
It's a place where little kid lies in his room and babbles
while blowing a nose balloon.
The sunlight sneaked over the threshold through
gap in Hanji could not be this pretty.

It's a mysterious place
Plum blossoms, orchids, chrysanthemuns and bamoo
blossoms
bloom and fall in Hanji flower bed.
The wind and sea of clouds flow through the muntins.
Through the hole in paper weather strip,
the flow of four seasons are in order.
It's a mysterious scenery

It's a place I miss
When I was young, I wonder where the kid went
Where he is now and what he's dreaming about.
I turn the activity photos of my memories upside down
and afterimages are coming in one after another

It's a place where snowflakes bloom.

In the yard and fence, red pums, yellow plums,
and white plums hold the snow wind and make snowflakes bloom.
A young girl comes out through a hole in the fence,
meets the naked boy and tells fable

It's a place where I dream.
As I climb bamboo forest path, it's filled with moonlight.
At the sound of my father's striking comb bamboo pyrography,
the phoenix that was chewing bamboo shoot files up,
the sound of Byeokodong Geomoongo playing is mysterious.

The pond is a place where monnlight shines.
Golden moon water falls as dew on lotus leaves.
and the starlight in the dew combines
and scatters galaxes.

Inside the silver-filled bongchang
is a kid's universe.

Bongchang : A window with small opening made for light and ventilation and sealed with paper(Hanji) without a window frame.
Hanji : Traditional Korean paper made of the bark of the paper mul berry tree & etc
Byeokodong : Firrniana simplex(or Parasol tree)
Geomungo : A Korean stringed instrument made of royal fox glove tree with six strings which are picked or flicked to make music.

One Dream

If only you and I oneday
meet in earnest love and
embroider one dream,
If our dreams could meet
and become a piece of carpet
I will wait.

After a long period of
silence and loneliness on a clod road
when one sadness gives a hand to another
and one ongoing looks into the deep eyes
of another longing
which winter wind
will make our love cold?

If only you and I could
meet one day after
a long lonely wait
and merge one dream
and one love.

Gobdani

Bukcheong water vendor's water carrier cutting through the dawn wind
Which alley in Bukchang-dong?
An alley that sells cold noodles and dumplings
When the full moon rises dung dung dung between creeping rafer of overstretched old house
The man,without delay, climbed onto her chest.

In the life window of munganbang where the 30 watt lamp was light,
if you throw a small stone
there was a beautiful person
who flew by crimson brocade skirt fluttering
and dimples in full moon.

Opening the creaky side door in sunset light
and heard her come in,
he clumsily wiped wet hands on his padded hatbaji
and ran out of kitchen of the room
deeper than the valley of her breasts
and when she came in blooming white like azalea flowers

there was an innocent man who received her a fruit bag.

The waning moon is setting on Mt. Mokmyeon.
It's a gloomy day as if snowflakes are falling
Because of longing that is coming in from farway,
I forgot to loss freshness of coffee
and run in one step, calling out to mountains on the eaves, setting up a folding screen
and directing a white naked body with layered clouds
I have had such a sneaky, sweet first love.

Dung dung dung : The shape of the rising sun
Munganbang : A small room located next to the gate of traditional Korean house
Hatbaji : Traditional Korean man's cotton-padded trousers for winter

One Dream

If only you and I one day
meet in earnest love and
embroider one dream,
If our dreams could meet
and become a piece of carpet
I will wait.

After a long period of
silence and loneliness on a clod road
when one sadness gives a hand to another
and one ongoing looks into the deep eyes
of another longing
which winter wind
will make our love cold?

If only you and I could
meet one day after
a long lonely wait
and merge one dream
and one love.

Unstoppable Love

In my hollow heart
a mouth-opened smile was put on it
and it turned into round moon.

In my empty, round moon heart
a overflowed dimpling was put on it
and it became a lake

On the round moon submerged in the lake
I put a sweet lip
and moon flower bloomed

He, He, I really can't stop
The moon flower on the lake is your face.

What should we do
with our unstoppable love?

He, He : A word imitating the sound or describing the motion of laughing loudly with a round, open mounth

Primitive Love

Everything that stays with us through time
Is truly a moment.

A fleeting light
leaves only a greater trace and
disappears into a past space-time
that can not be summoned.

Thinking about this,
I don't know how to protect the difficult love
that I am struggling to endure now.

Free emotions intervene.
Don't bind yourself too deeply
There's no need to be afraid.
Love wherever your heart goes
Just love.

Moon Bruce

On a night when the leaves are wet with dew
on a entwined bamboo forest road past Wandonggol
Ganadang.
follows me and whispers,
then sits down on thatched wall

When I open twig gate, starlight follow me in
and sit down the bamboo bench
but you take a peek
and then turn away in a cold breeze.

In the early evening , moonlight shines on River Yeongsan
and before you know it, you are turning he pagoda
of hoguk temple.
Temple bell is weeping at the heart breaking story.

A strong wind blows through guardian tree of Wandong gol
Your shadow crossing cloud bridge carrying a backpack
becomes even more lonely

Please pour moon water on Lee family's rain-fed rice
fields

and at down, enjoy a few cup of bamboo liquor with white mangtae much room gueen in the bamboo grove of Kim family
and I can't see you blooming with love.

I am the protagonist of tragedy
Even though I am heartbreaking loneliness
pricked by a tangerine thorn, I miss you and

Wandonggol Ganadong : a place name
Manftae mushroom : Dictyophora indusiate Fisch

Sad Love

If I hug the back of the past years and greet them.
Why did you secretly leave me behind?
The unforgettable image of you brings tears to my eyes
and I wrap them around the thread drum

I cut the fabric from the moonlight that fell in the bamboo forest.
I made clothes for you according to the look of longing
I pick stars that have fallen every dew and sew them onto your clothes.

The longing for you flows on the pitch-black night clouds
that have set moon, and I go and go without knowing,
But you are far away, distant and distant in the sky
My anxiety is deep and I wander through the swamps of floating grass.

Waning Moon

When the wind and rain hit, I fall alone
I, who only loved a single star flower, was the protagonist of
tragedy, Now, it is useless, so I will shake off my wings.

I will empty out all the desires that were filled up
From the arrogant eyes that tried to be eternal to empty eyes,
I will now turn back.
I will cross that forbidden diagonal line that confines the night.

I still dream
The full moon that hides in the flower stream and is delivered of a baby
The color of the water that was expected to bloom for a thousand years is fading away.

Ah~sad compassion
Let me empty this harsh attachment
Let me out off the spreading longing

Do not return that love.
On the outing road where I stayed for a whiles
My eyes wet with the delicate light of the morning star
and let the wind sigh and set along with sunset
everywhere.

To the constellation I left the nest
let my back be dignified as I return
Crossing the phenomenal world, climb up the peak,
I can climb over the wall of perception.

I love the star flower. The sorrow that accompanied it
draw a line and mark on that forbidden wall
that confines the meaning less substance and try to
confine my life and hide it in the space and time of
a state of enlightment

Let the vain desires that flutter with lonely wings
and the delicate eyes that pass way to the constellations
of the mother sky
become a sacred provocation!

Waning Moon

When the wind and rain hit,I fall alone
I, who only loved a single star flower, was the protagonist of
tragedy, Now, it is useless, so I will shake off my wings.

I will empty out all the desires that were filled up
From the arrogant eyes that tried to be eternal to empty eyes,
I will now turn back.
I will cross that forbidden diagonal line that confines the night.

I still dream
The full moon that hides in the flower stream and is delivered of a baby
The color of the water that was expected to bloom for a thousand years is fading away.

Ah~sad compassion
Let me empty this harsh attachment
Let me out off the spreading longing
Do not return that love.

On the outing road where I stayed for a whiles
My eyes wet with the delicate light of the morning star
and let the wind sigh and set along with sunset
everywhere.

To the constellation I left the nest
let my back be dignified as I return
Crossing the phenomenal world, climb up the peak,
I can climb over the wall of perception.

I love the star flower. The sorrow that accompanied it
draw a line and mark on that forbidden wall
that confines the meaning less substance and try to
confine my life and hide it in the space and time of
a state of enlightment

Let the vain desires that flutter with lonely wings
and the delicate eyes that pass way to the constellations
of the mother sky
become a sacred provocation!

Creative Love

The world's relationship between men and women
will be no perfect combination from the beginning

As we live,
we empty space that is full of each other
and expand the spaces that are lacking
and filling the empty spaces

There is only a well-matched relationship
that is created later rather than
a good relationship.
True love is like this…

Part 5
The Reason Yew Trees Have Survived for 2,000 Years

Baby

When you first come to me,
Did you know that wind brought you?
Did you know that clouds brought you?
Did you know that sun planted the spark of life?

With that frame,
when your heart starts to moving,
you grow up with hope for the distant future
and with just your bright smile,
did you know your father forget all his anxieties?

You are my everything,
You are one universe.
Oh! my baby!

My son was born a week ago. He is a handsome guy with a sharp nose.
As a child who I got late, I feel the whole world and so happy that I
write a poem even if it is not enough.

Hometown

Nostalgic imagination

Cosmos haneul haneul
and dyed sky blue.

The dragonfly binggeul binggeul like seeker
It ripes red

With all my longing
I play hide and seek every night
and trace traces in my dream.

My hometown, a distant hometown
is a hundred year flower bamboo-dew liquor's
drinking house!

Haneul haneul : lighltly: flutteringly
-In the manner of drooping feebly
and waying lightly, repeatedly
Binggeul bingeul : A word describing one repeatedly
moving in large cirle

It's a Thatched Nest

Putting soybean paste in the sunlight
under the earthen wall, Korea mint's leaf red skirt
flutters
A lonely mean cottage beyond the hill

golden grass painted in gold on blue paper is sleeping
because she like the sun.

The chilly wind insisted that it was a guest.
It beats the pungent scent of mugwort and goes back
to the vegetable garden
Cold, deep water rapids under pebble stair,
hugging the stepping stones
it's pouring tears

A wonderful spring day
Peach blossoms, forsythia flower, azalea flower,
floating flowers dung dung dung,
the sunlight that traveled hundreds of millions of light years
spilits the grass land and
the morning dew filled with moon water
shines brightly

The Sound of Bier

If you go now, when will you come?
Bukmang mountain is in front of my house.

Sleep, sleep, sleep
ehe eheee, let's go with you, with you, with you

Even coffin bearers who soothes the dead are sad
Even mountains, rivers and tress weep at the sorrowful
And heartrending sound of weeping
The bell sound of singer on bier railing
ddaenggeureong ddaenggeureng ddaenggeureng
In the sound of a singer whp smoothes the dead,
the hearts of mouners left behind are broken

The person going to Bukmangsancheon
let put down all your worries and take it easy on your way,
take a ride on the small boat that is floating above the clouds
go to Bukmangsancheon without hesitation
Loud weeoing sound is very, very sad

The bier flowers are sprinkled on the way to the dead
The bier goes around the dead's birth home and
in the spound of the bier-carriers, the bier dancing and playing
Those who are connected to the daed are sad and sad,
They weep along with the bier

Hitting the ground, leaving me, leaving us behind,
if you go now, when will you come back?,
what will we do, If you don't come? they are crying loudly
As bell sound of singer urges the way, the soul of dead
Head helplessly towards its hometown, the distance universe

Sleep, sleep, sleep
Ehehe eheee let's go with you, with you, you…

Bukmangsan / Bukmangsanchen : A place where people are buried after death
Ehe Ehe ee : A sound that help the energy along with song or beat

Childhood Friend

When I was kid,
In the reed field on a autumn days,
childhood friends who played and
rolled around and picked reed.

Standing in the golden light,
childhood games were
the source of pure beginnings

Recalling and reminiscing about this
is the source and self-discipline that restores
the distorted emotions of people who have been
immersed in the murky urban culture.

Today, I meet my elementary school class mates
I miss you, guys
Wait!

Mother Is Getting Married

Mother is getting married
Pure and pure love, more beautiful than flowers
follows her bridegroom.
Taking a make up and riding in flower palanquin(Gama)
She is coming to get married to handsome husband.

The day the pomegranates were red and bursting open
The late-sleeping yeonhwadang lady who set up a flower stalk,
was jealous coldly, when the flower palanquin came in.
The pomegranates family set closely together and greeted
The bride through the crack in the door.
The hawfinch spread the news to the neighborhood
They sat on the gingo tree in a group
and held a celebration party.

'At the bride's beautiful appearance coming down from the flower palanquin, the gloom's mouth opens wide. The scholars in the green bamboo forest were delighted and with a grass of bamboo wine at banguet table, they spontaneously recite Sijochang.

Gama : A small house shaped transpotation means, held by two or four people with a passenger inside

Sijochang : A song sung without accompaniment and accompanied by a set melody in a three-part format established during Chosun Dynasty

Oh My Heaven!

Oh! my Heaven!
Please embrace my palpitating crab mentality
and give me a throbbing
unrequited love.

Oh! my Heaven!
Please embrace the blazing magma
and cool down
the sweltering heat

Oh! my Heaven!
Please hold my white, burning
Breast and dry up
the swaying water clolor.

Flower

Precious
Love
is
fragrant
flower
that
is
born
and
blooms
in
the
universe.

One Dream

To give you a present
I went fishing in the Galaxy River.
I tried to catch a pretty star
Sitting by the river where countries stars swim
I threw the fishing rod
I tried to tempt Cassiopia and the little bear
It even scares scorpions
I prayed for the Seven Stars
but it was just one dream, I only got a shooting star.

I miss you
I launched a small boat and rowed in the sea of stars
I tried to catch a pretty heart
Riding on the flower and the water scales
I split the water color
so close to touch but so far away
Starflower fell
It was just one dream, only spring sentiments was caught.

Solitude

On days when I miss you, I write poetry
On days when I miss you, I drink alcohol
and walked the forest path I walked with you

Still, on days when I miss you
I step on fallen leaves that burn the embers
I woke you up by burning my longing

[Samteo Quotations]

Saemteo Quotations
Solitude is meditating and healing a philosophical thought.

Fishmen's Hope

The bleak twilight is prolonged.
The sound of grass bugs is loud
and eagle owl looks pitiful.

What shall we do with this?
Shall we drop the anchor and cast the net?
In the love play of foxes at the streamside,
The reed leaves trembled and is frightened

Who can believes in the innocence of reed?
It's a flower that blooms and falls
Love and farewell bloom and fall endlessly
The sound of shaking wind cuts my heart.

What shall we do with this?
Shall we raise the net?
Shall we let go all of longing that we have gathered up?
What if it is an empty net?

After empty it all,
Shall we save the round smile
that glows red at down?

The clouds are gone, the moon is setting
the sound of grass bug is loud,
scops owl feel sad

Moonlight Serenade

When the sunset dies, the moonlight sprouts
wets Eungabi in Mirinae's star field, bursts star flowers
and flirtatious eyes throw it sparkly

The oxidized sunset moans sweep away space and time
fills the unfocused silence
The owl serenade is beautiful and sad night,
The blue eyes of the supia owl illuminate the silence

The secret world flows and another moonlight
fills an auspicious cloud
Oppressive soul wet silver wave
Dazed heart fill love
A pressed chest
Would it be okay to throw it?

Coexistence

The coexistence and harmony of
nature and humans is
a harmonious blessing
and
the love
that bloom within it
is a beautiful
and legendary flower.

Contradiction

Between coldness and passion
Isn't it a constant coming and going?

Although it seems cold
with passion in it
it's full too.
Even when it comes to passion
calmness is another emotion.
Could it be hiding?

Perhaps
we don't need love,
isn't that what we need from a sincere person?
Love isn't it like that?
Perhaps.

Coincidence point

I don't want love to be emotional
Because I have to look at more delicate place than that
It's like threading a camel through a narrow door
that can't give everything.
To lift up even the weakest fallen grass,
I needed love.

You are the ideal, I am the reality
In the front of the gab between reality and logic,
I hope that we, the weakest,
will become one.

Language of tears

In a difficult life,
the language of hot tears
shed by a loving lover
is true language that
moistens a dry heart
and a tired soul,
a heartfelt confession
and a language of
sincere love.

Silent Life

When I think about something
and pick up the pen, it disappears.

The silent cry that overwhelms the cooperation of
thorough general view blooms a gorgeous glower
in the midst of nothingness

The inability to see the distant, silent, hidden specs
comes as a pity.

and we forget this extreme generosity
that should be accomplished by me, not me.

and I only go around the remote alleys
covered by the full ness of reality.

What you can't get
is no longer ours.

Spring flowers that bloomed in full glory
blame only spring wind that brushes their faces.

There is no reason for us to blame things
around us like this

Hunger

The rain comes
to appease
the emotional hunger
in my heart.

Missing you is
a sign that I want
to fill my empty heart
with your love

Nameless Dump Flower

A flower that can not speak,but when you hold key and approach it with strong magic and open its flower bud
It opens a bundle of stories of long-time love
A woman who has no name and can not speak
,hits the night dew with her delicate breath
Living and living!, blooms and fall!
I like it because it's a mountain, I like it because it's a water
A pitiful flower of sorrow that digs up star glowers and plants
them in the moon field
let's embrace it gently with the moonlight.
Aridongdong, my love!

Aridongdong : Originated from Arirang, a Korean fork song and Dongdong meaning "joy"

Dreamlike Love

A flower with a beautiful smile,
A flower that blooms like hasy mist
in a dream
In one wish where dreams of hope bloom,
happiness is stored
I bow my head and wait.

Oh flower that pace around beautifully
I breathe my soul into your stamens
I am moving lightly on the state of no-self
Waiting is also a beautiful blessing

A flower that seeps into the mist.
I want to seep you p in my dreams,
and break you so that you are crushed,
my love flower

A Letter Written in Silence

You have lowered the curtains of your heart today
and I am pacing in front of you.
How long will I have to linger in front of your door?

By the time you lift the curtains of your heart
I have put up a huge wall
When the unsophisticated times pierce my heart
and a cold wind blows

By the time you in dream lower the curtain of your heart
I write a letter to the quiet wall of silence,
asking if I can love you.

The Reason Yew Trees Have Survived for 2,000 Years

For example, the word silently uttered by passing wind
Would not have been profound legend.

That tree is in the right place
I mean, a thousand years
Grandfather, grandfather, grandfather, gradfather,
From the time of the grandfather dozens of generations ago,
the root are planted in the heart of earth and sky is spread out
When the stars open jureongjureong,
It's eating them up

It must have spoken nonsense that was thrown openly as if was nothing special.
Roll clouds spread out a mat and sat down
And it must have just been a matter of giving advice.

That's right, that guy is right place where he should be
A thousand years in life, a thousand years in dead
He is live aloofly, holding onto the thin thread of his life

Even if he dies, he is not dead
He doesn't feel unfair

Let's have an affair with another woman.
Don't commit incest, and if you had sex with another woman with good genes,
then one side of your body wouldn't have rotted away like that
You could easily live another two or three thousand years!

That's right, he lived for two thousand years
and couldn't have still stayed
But there was a time when he lived with fresh
If he stayed still, he wouldn't be a legend
If he didn't open his dull eyes and say something like that, he would have been upset

"You, who are born and disappear all the time and have no existence,
What do you know and preach about?
Even so, you have to live at least two thousand years to know the life of a tree.
If you die, don't die suddenly
You die slowly while observing nature inaction and controlling your breathing
Only then you can under stand the province of nature

and profound meaning of heaven
Experiencing life and death in one place
is pure love and art.

Who will record of the gossip of those who are
teeming with one voice?
Whether it is a tale or legend, when that two thousand year
guy crosses the death line, those around him
would not have thought of it.
He drew strokes and dots on the forbidden wall of
the material world, imprisoning him for the rest of his lifes
moving to the absolute world,
it must have been a gamble and a friend who improves
the Tao together.

SAEMMOON 1054

The love I met on the trail
Lee Jung-rok 9th Poetry Collection

Issue_Nov. 1, 2024
Printing_Nov. 1, 2024
Publisher_Saemmoon Book Publishing
Author_Lee Jung-rok
Editing advisor_Lee Geun-bae, Kim So-yeop, Son Hae-il
Planning_Park Hoon-sik
Translator_Parl Choong-ryeol
Design_Shin Sun-ok, Han Ga-eul
Printing_Saemmoon Book Publishing

Address_56 101gil Dongil-ro Jungnang-gu, Seoul, Korea
Telephone_02-491-0060 / 02-491-0096
Fax_02-491-0040
E-mail_rok9539@daum.net / saemteonews@naver.com
Website_www.saemmoon.co.kr(Saem Literature)
        www.saemmoonnews.co.kr(Saemmoon News)
Publisher Registration_2019-26
Business Registration_113-82-76122
Saemmoon Literature Lifelong Educatin Center(Online Remote)-
Officially approved by Department of Education_320193122
Saemmoon Literature Lifelong Education Center(Offline)-
Officially approved by Department of Education_320203133

ISBN_979-11-94325-83-3

The formation of this poetry collection follows the author's intention.
Copyright of this book belongs to the author and Saemmoon.
Reprinting, plagiarism, and reproduction are strictly limited.

We offer an exchange of damaged books at the place of your purchase.
This book complies with the code of ethics and practice by the Korean publication ethics committee